MW01474234

YOU ARE THE LIGHT OF THE WORLD
By Murray Hack

Copyright © Murray Hack 2008

ISBN-10: 1-897373-58-9
ISBN-13: 978-1-897373-58-3

All rights reserved. No part of this publication may be reproduced, stored in a retrieval system, or transmitted in any form or by any means—electronic, mechanical, photocopy, recording, or any other—except for brief quotations in printed reviews, without prior permission from the publisher.

Scripture taken from the HOLY BIBLE, NEW INTERNATIONAL VERSION®. Copyright © 1973, 1978, 1984 International Bible Society. Used by permission of Zondervan. All rights reserved.

Printed by Word Alive Press
131 Cordite Road, Winnipeg, Manitoba, Canada R3W 1S1

WORD ALIVE PRESS

SOULS HARBOUR RESCUE MISSION

www.soulsharbourrescuemission.org

Souls Harbour RESCUE Mission is an inner city ministry located in Regina, Saskatchewan, Canada. We exist to rescue people from poverty, addiction, and sin by providing emergency help such as food, clothing, and shelter, life-changing discipleship programs and the Gospel Message.

Souls Harbour RESCUE Mission is able to provide a full continuum of care for the least, the last and the lost. For those on the streets we serve meals at our soup kitchen, hand out free clothing from the clothing store, and provide a free place to sleep at our emergency shelter. Those seeking more long-term help can join our LifeChange Discipleship Program, a year-long program for men and women with life-controlling problems and addictions. And for those seeking a healthy, supportive Christian community, we have an inner city church as well as low-income housing.

We are on a RESCUE Mission to bring homeless, addicted and hurting people into a Souls Harbour of love, faith and a new life.

All proceeds from this book go towards funding the many ministries of Souls Harbour RESCUE Mission. May you be blessed by the Lord, the Maker of heaven and earth. Psalm 115:15

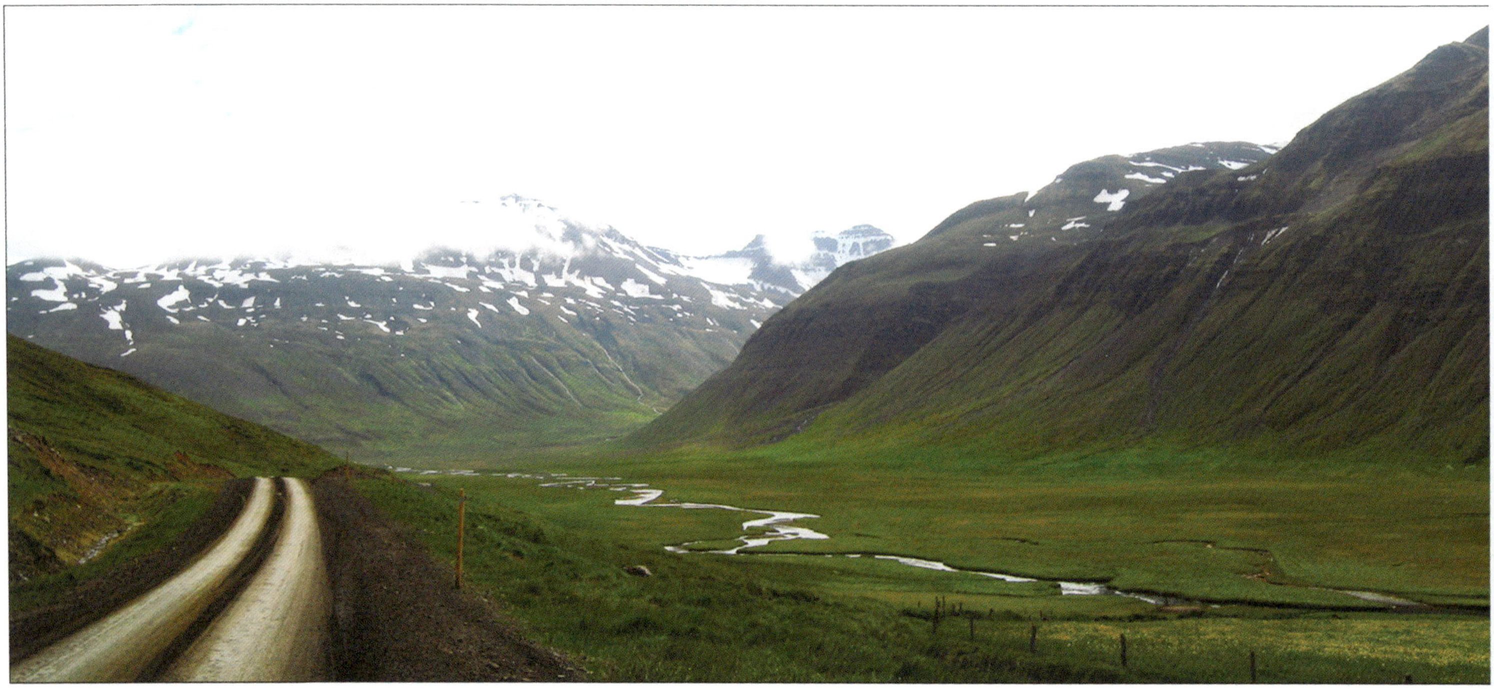

But small is the gate and narrow the road that leads to life, and only a few find it.

Matthew 7:14

For God, who said, "Let light shine out of darkness," made his light shine in our hearts to give us the light of the knowledge of the glory of God in the face of Christ.

2 Corinthians 4:6

Who shall separate us from the love of Christ? Shall trouble or hardship or persecution or famine or nakedness or danger or sword?

Romans 8:35

Why, you do not even know what will happen tomorrow. What is your life? You are a mist that appears for a little while and then vanishes.

James 4:14

Deep calls to deep in the roar of your waterfalls; all your waves and breakers have swept over me.

Psalm 42:7

"...Why do you stand here looking into the sky? This same Jesus, who has been taken from you into heaven, will come back in the same way you have seen him go into heaven."

Acts 1:11

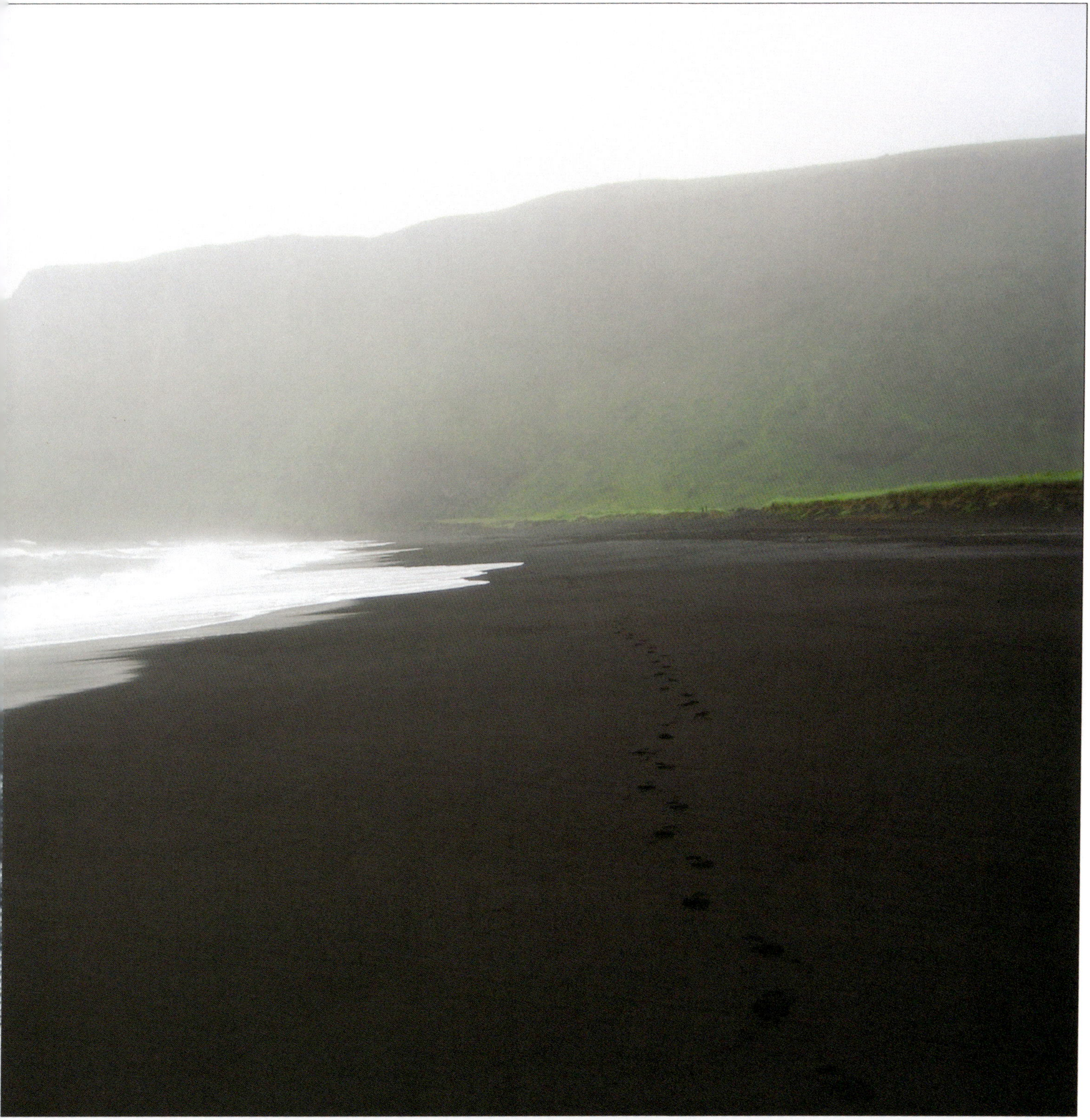

Splendor and majesty are before him; strength and joy in his dwelling place.

1 Chronicles 16:27

Who may ascend the hill of the LORD? Who may stand in his holy place?

Psalm 24:3

Charm is deceptive, and beauty is fleeting; but a woman who fears the LORD is to be praised.

Proverbs 31:30

He searches the sources of the rivers and brings hidden things to light.

Job 28:11

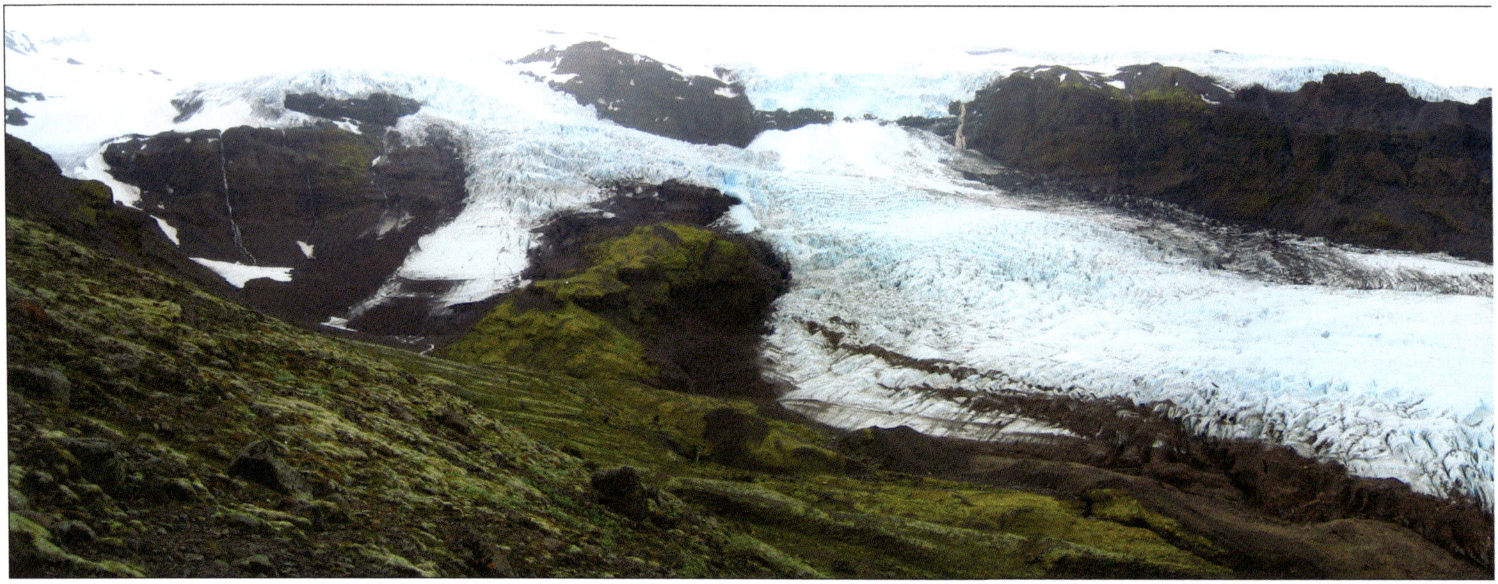

Then the sovereignty, power and greatness of the kingdoms under the whole heaven will be handed over to the saints, the people of the Most High. His kingdom will be an everlasting kingdom, and all rulers will worship and obey him.

Daniel 7:27

Let my teaching fall like rain and my words descend like dew, like showers on new grass, like abundant rain on tender plants.

Deuteronomy 32:2

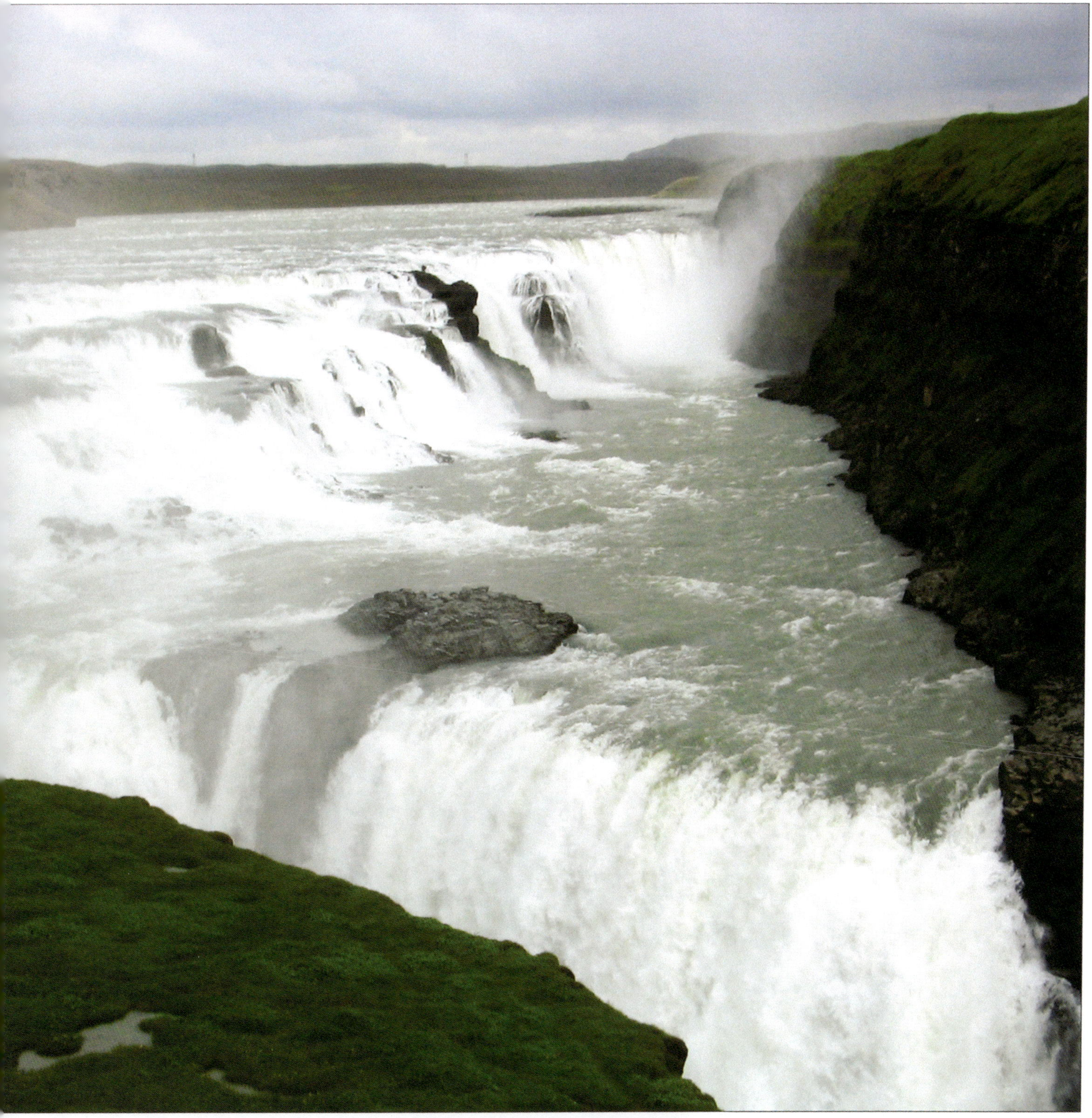

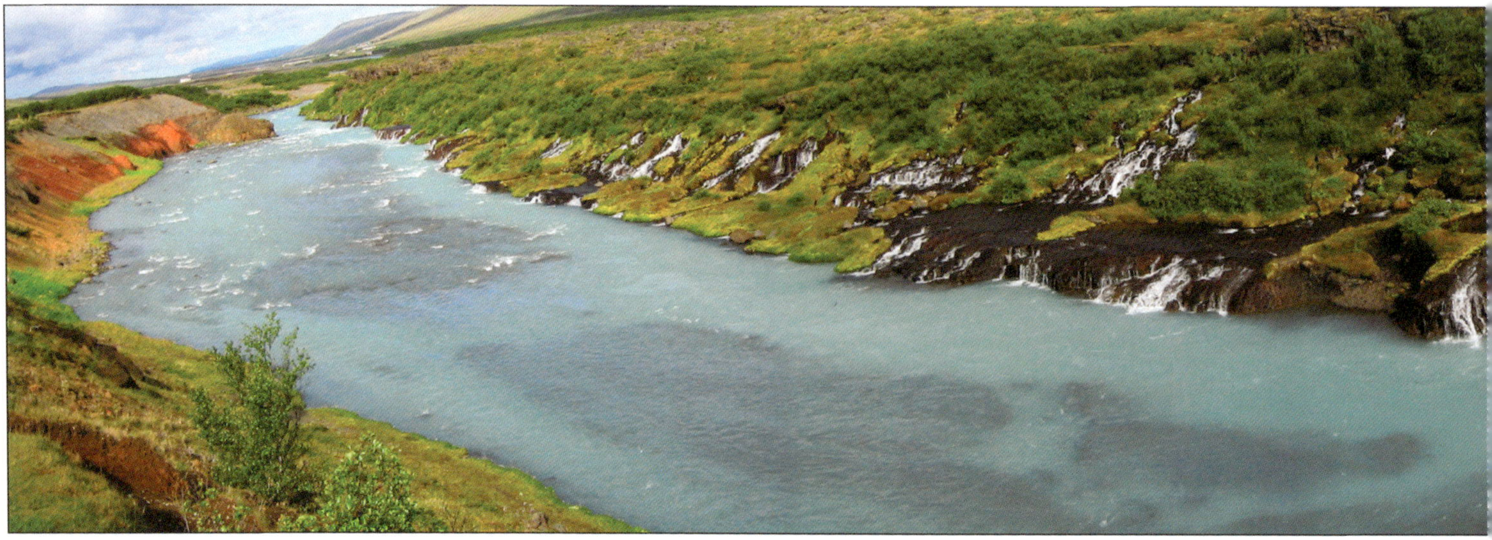

Then the angel showed me the river of the water of life, as clear as crystal, flowing from the throne of God and of the Lamb.

Revelation 22:1

"Be still, and know that I am God; I will be exalted among the nations, I will be exalted in the earth."

Psalm 46:10

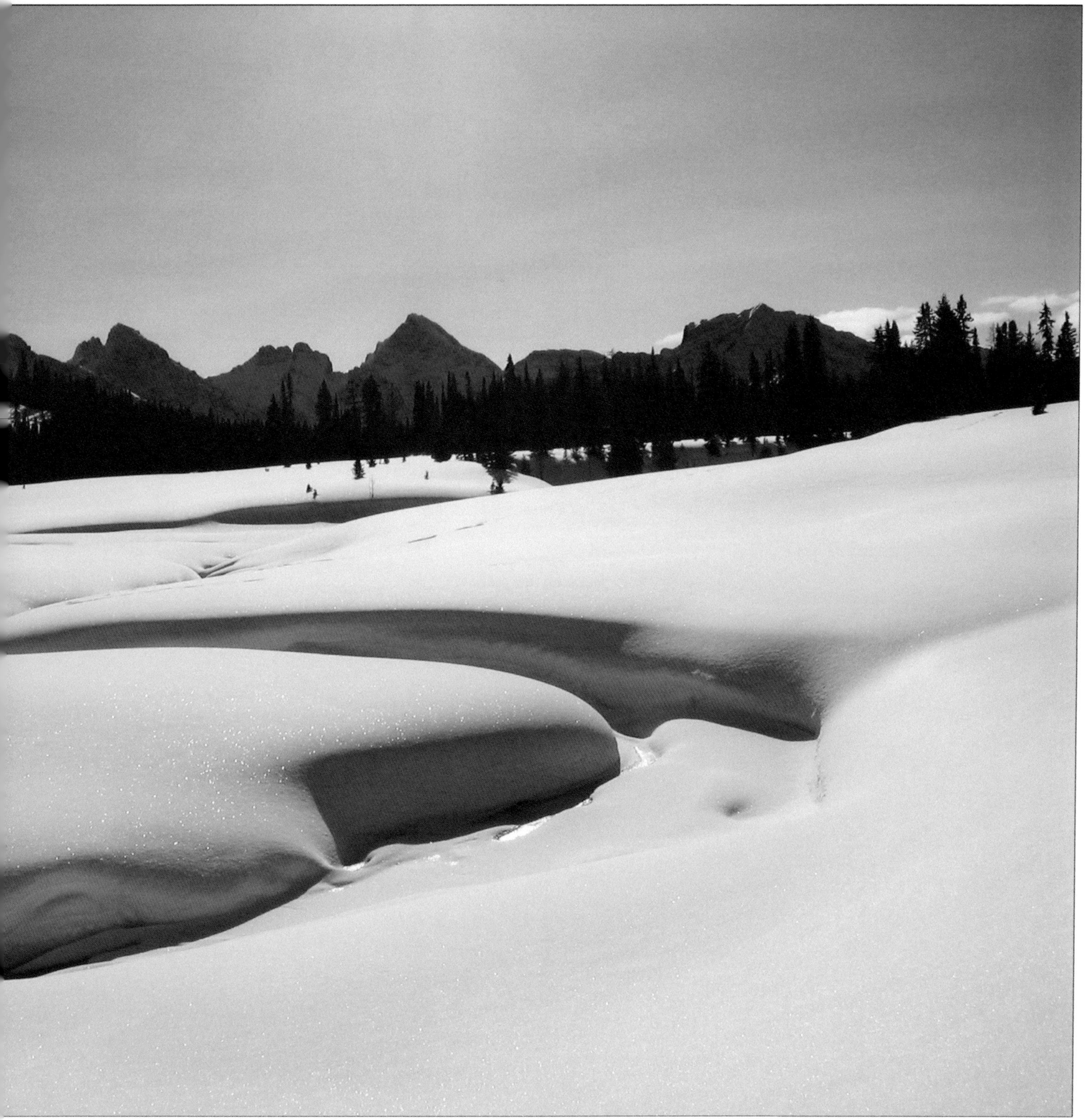

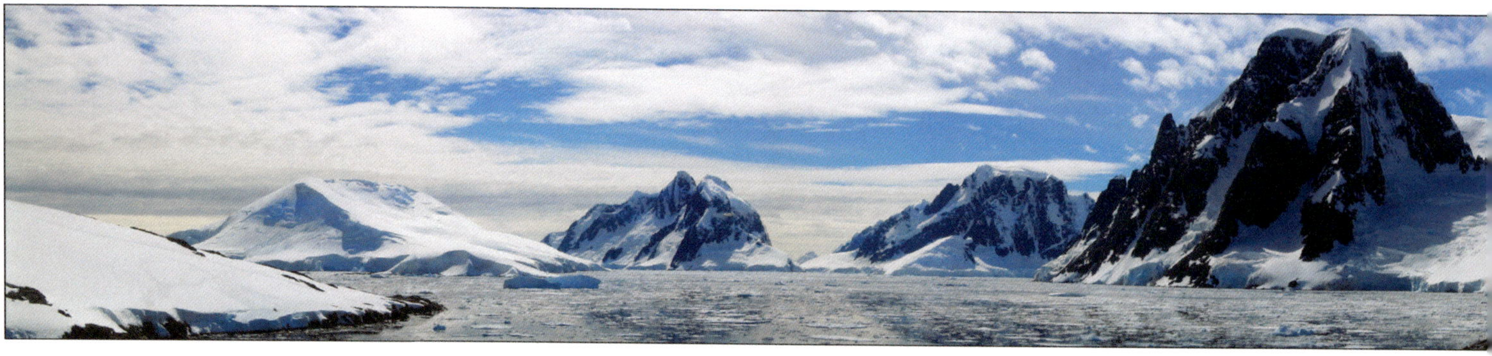

From Zion, perfect in beauty, God shines forth.

Psalm 50:2

You live in the midst of deception.

Jeremiah 9:6

The mountains melt like wax before the LORD, before the Lord of all the earth.

Psalm 97:5

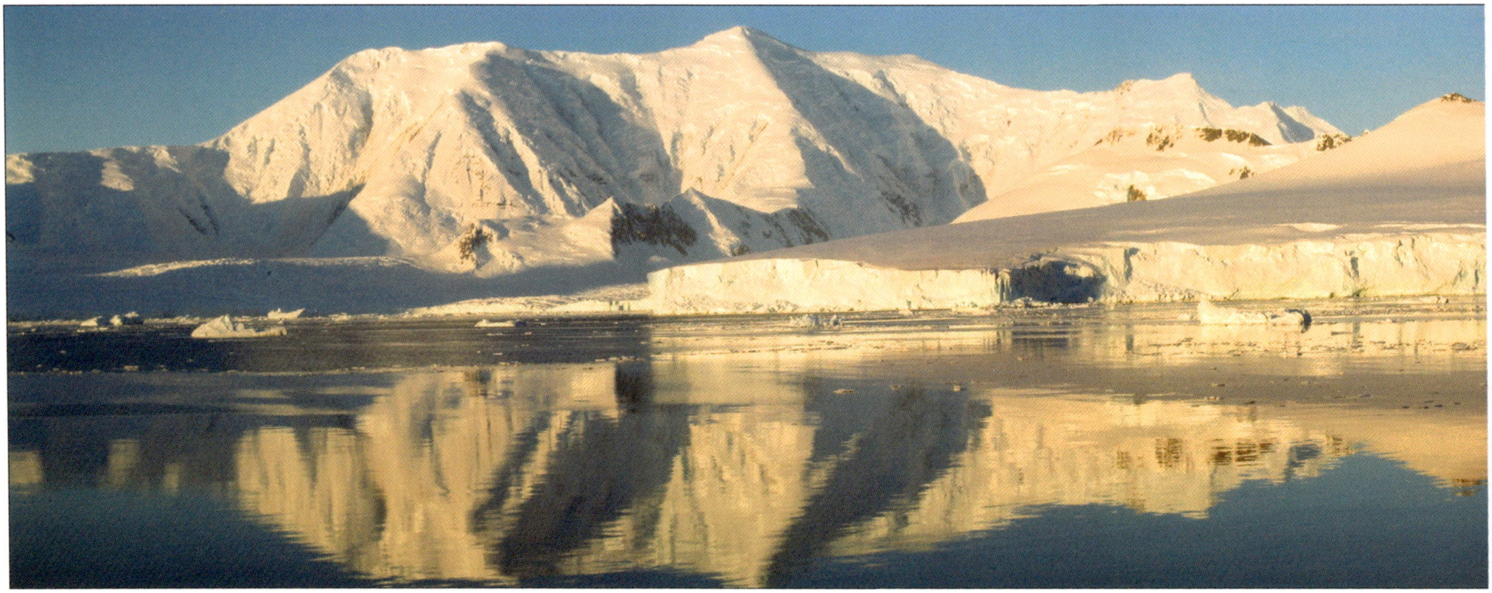

And we, who with unveiled faces all reflect the Lord's glory, are being transformed into his likeness with ever-increasing glory, which comes from the Lord, who is the Spirit.

2 Corinthians 3:18

The curtain of the temple was torn in two from top to bottom.

Mark 15:38

The breath of God produces ice, and the broad waters become frozen.

Job 37:10

The people walking in darkness have seen a great light; on those living in the land of the shadow of death a light has dawned.

Isaiah 9:2

You are all sons of the light and sons of the day. We do not belong to the night or to the darkness.

1 Thessalonians 5:5

It shone with the glory of God, and its brilliance was like that of a very precious jewel, like a jasper, clear as crystal.

Revelation 21:11

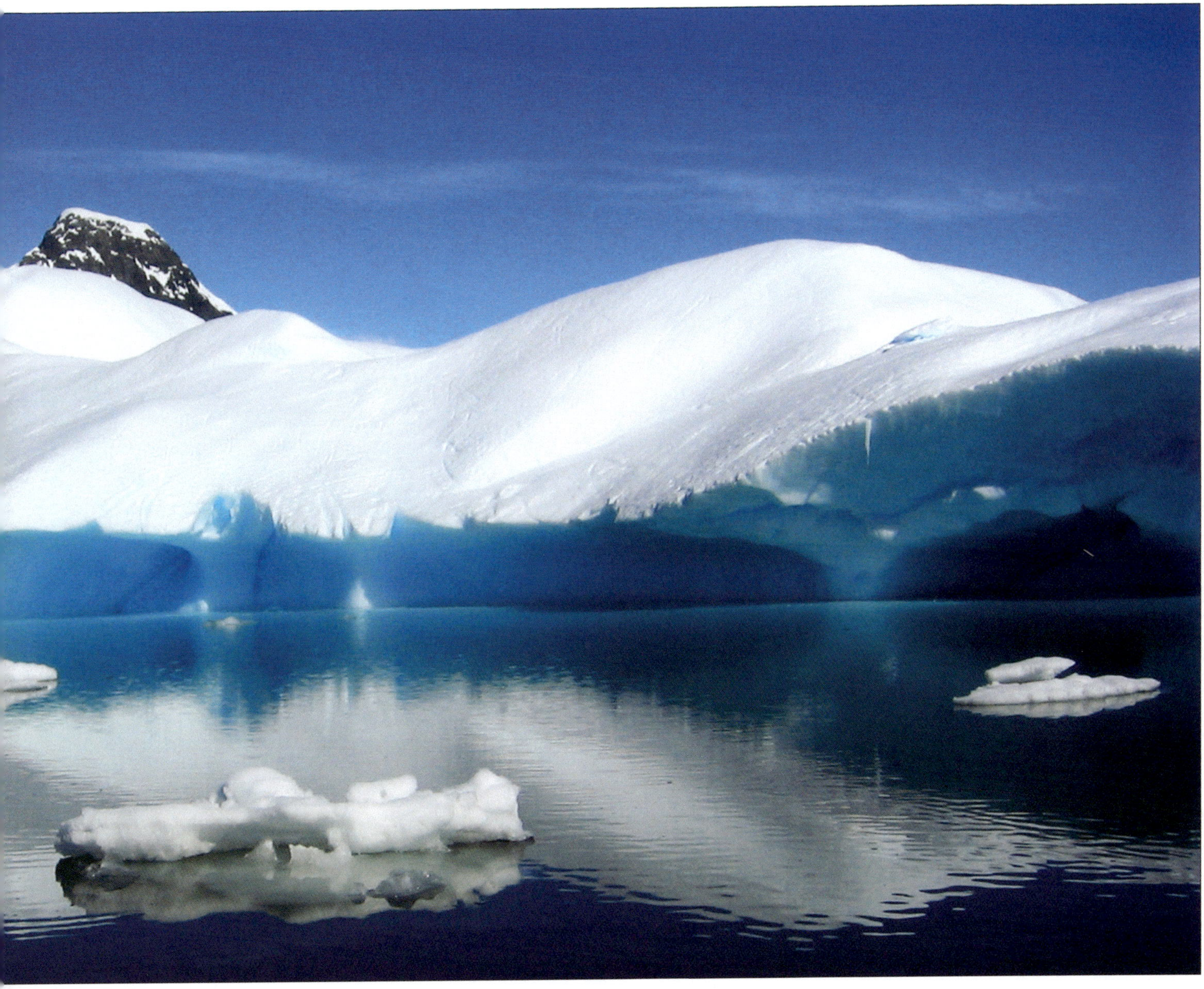

"Where, O death, is your victory? Where, O death, is your sting?"

1 Corinthians 15:55

It will be a unique day, without daytime or nighttime- a day known to the LORD. When evening comes, there will be light.

Zechariah 14:7

Blessed is the man who perseveres under trial, because when he has stood the test, he will receive the crown of life that God has promised to those who love him.

James 1:12

Therefore everyone who hears these words of mine and puts them into practice is like a wise man who built his house on the rock.

Matthew 7:24

In him and through faith in him we may approach God with freedom and confidence.

Ephesians 3:12

Jesus said, "My kingdom is not of this world. If it were, my servants would fight to prevent my arrest by the Jews. But now my kingdom is from another place."

John 18:36

God decided in advance to adopt us into his own family by bringing us to himself through Jesus Christ. This is what he wanted to do, and it gave him great pleasure.

Ephesians 1:5

For everyone born of God overcomes the world. This is the victory that has overcome the world, even our faith.

1 John 5:4

Jesus replied, "Foxes have holes and birds of the air have nests, but the Son of Man has no place to lay his head."

Matthew 8:20

"I will refresh the weary and satisfy the faint."

Jeremiah 31:25

"Enter through the narrow gate. For wide is the gate and broad is the road that leads to destruction, and many enter through it. But small is the gate and narrow the road that leads to life, and only a few find it."

Matthew 7:13-14

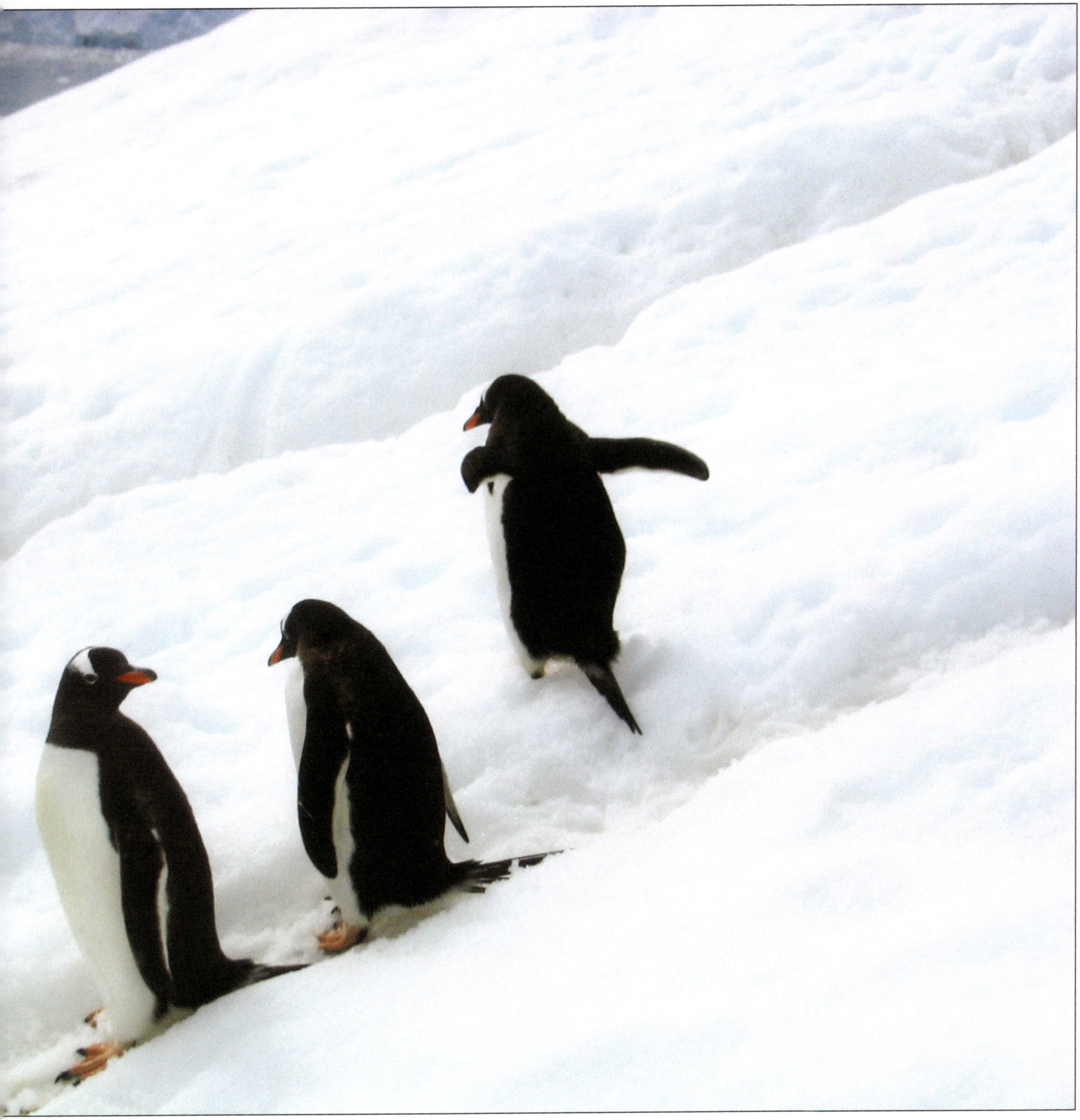

He let loose the east wind from the heavens
and led forth the south wind by his power.

Psalm 78:26

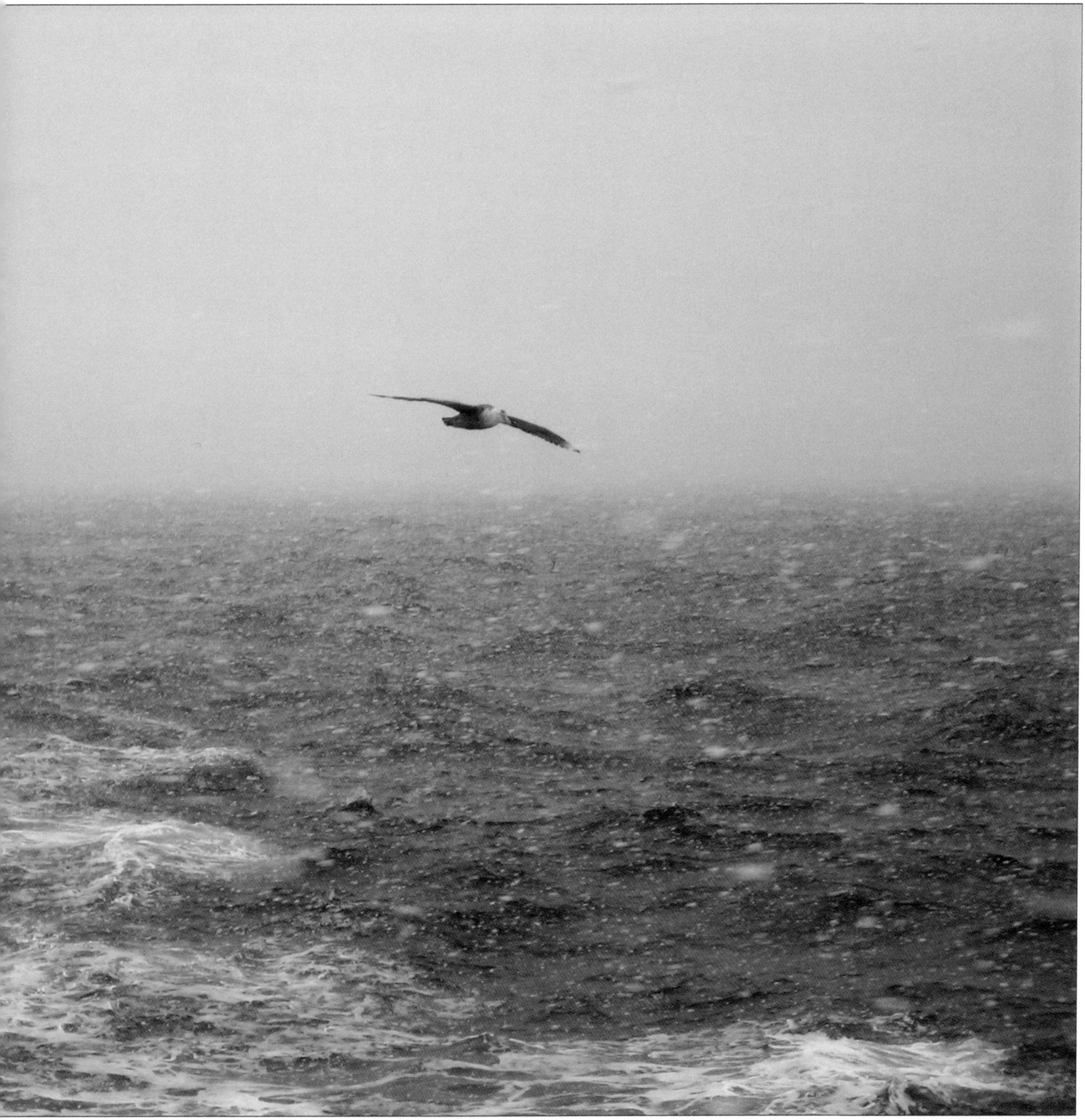

There the ships go to and fro, and the leviathan, which you formed to frolic there.

Psalm 104:26

He alone has spread out the heavens and marches on the waves of the sea.

Job 9:8

In his hand is the life of every creature and the breath of all mankind.

Job 12:10

He reveals deep and mysterious things and knows what lies hidden in darkness, though he is surrounded by light.

Daniel 2:22

How delightful is your love, my sister, my bride! How much more pleasing is your love than wine, and the fragrance of your perfume than any spice!

Song of Solomon 4:10

You may fight the good fight, holding on to faith and a good conscience. Some have rejected these and so have shipwrecked their faith.

1 Timothy 1:18b-19

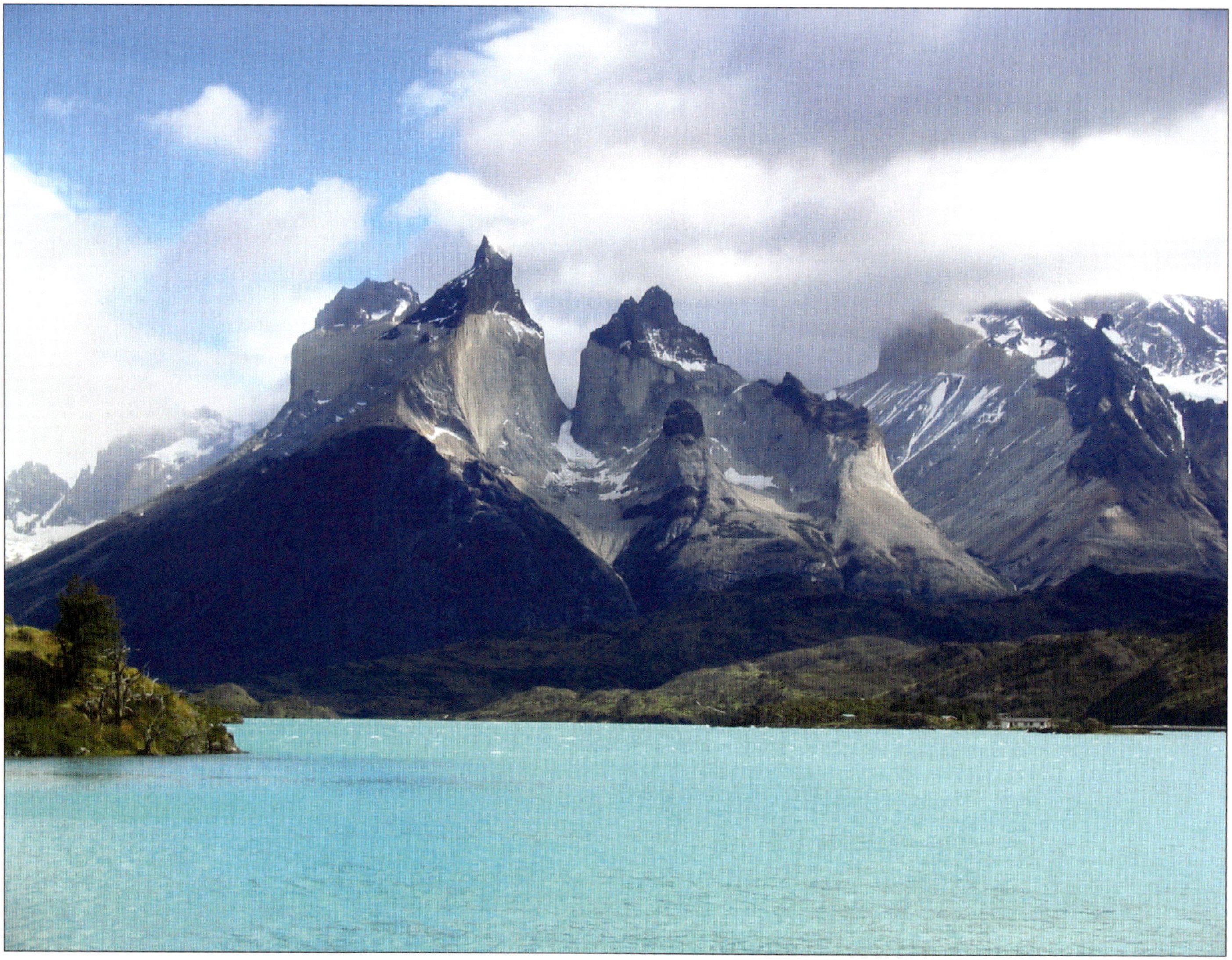

I will cut off the horns of all the wicked, but the horns of the righteous will be lifted up.

Psalm 75:10

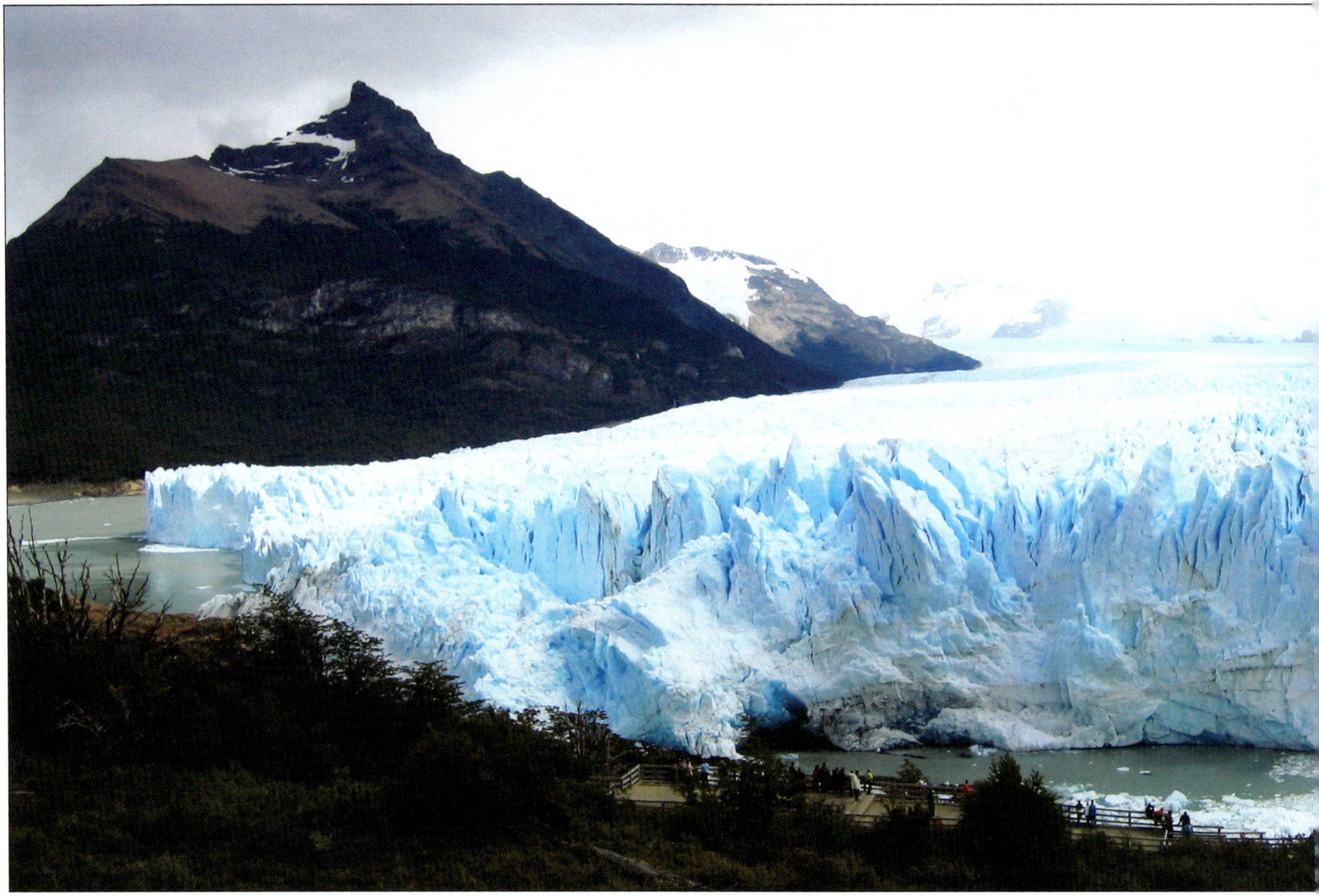

For he himself is our peace, who has made the two one and has destroyed the barrier, the dividing wall of hostility.

Ephesians 2:14

I saw the Holy City, the new Jerusalem, coming down out of heaven from God, prepared as a bride beautifully dressed for her husband.

Revelation 21:2

Jesus replied, "I tell you the truth, if you have faith and do not doubt ... you can say to this mountain, 'Go, throw yourself into the sea,' and it will be done."

Matthew 21:21

Do not let the oppressed retreat in disgrace; may the poor and needy praise your name.

Psalm 74:21

That day will be a day of wrath, a day of distress and anguish, a day of trouble and ruin, a day of darkness and gloom, a day of clouds and blackness.

Zephaniah 1:15

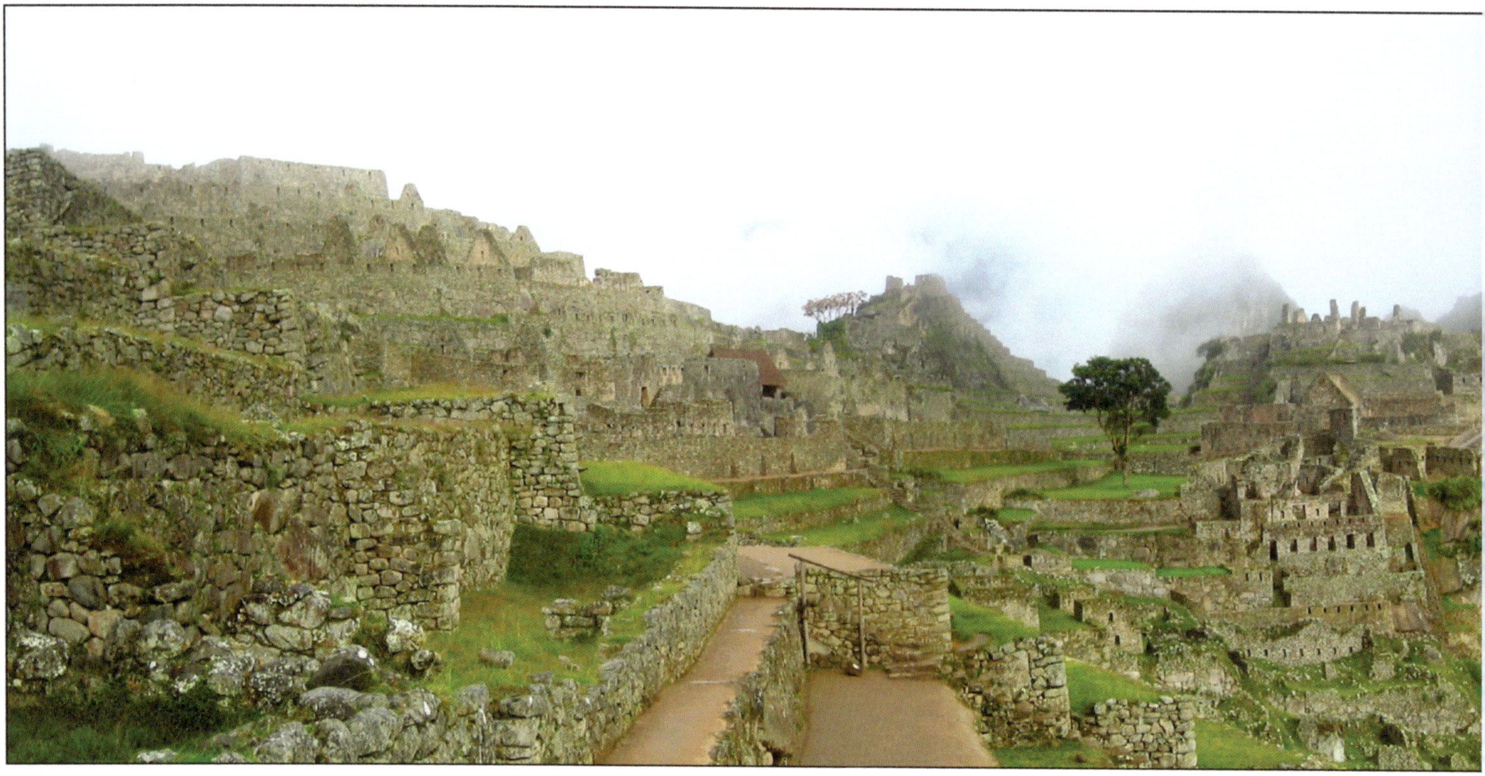

The kingdom of heaven is like treasure hidden in a field. When a man found it, he hid it again, and then in his joy went and sold all he had and bought that field.

Matthew 13:44

As soon as Jesus was baptized, he went up out of the water. At that moment heaven was opened, and he saw the Spirit of God descending like a dove and lighting on him.

Matthew 3:16

For as the soil makes the sprout come up and a garden causes seeds to grow, so the Sovereign LORD will make righteousness and praise spring up before all nations.

Isaiah 61:11

We blossom like a flower and then wither. Like a passing shadow, we quickly disappear.

Job 14:2

Flowers appear on the earth; the season of singing has come, the cooing of doves is heard in our land.

Song of Solomon 2:12

Spring up, O well! Yes, sing its praises!

Numbers 21:17

Be my rock of refuge, to which I can always go; give the command to save me, for you are my rock and my fortress.

Psalm 71:3

Like a horse in open country, they did not stumble.

Isaiah 63:13

"I have swept away your offenses like a cloud, your sins like the morning mist. Return to me, for I have redeemed you."

Isaiah 44:22

Better a meal of vegetables where there is love than a fattened calf with hatred.

Proverbs 15:17

Your statutes are my heritage forever; they are the joy of my heart.

Psalm 119:111

It was majestic in beauty, with its spreading boughs, for its roots went down to abundant waters.

Ezekiel 31:7

"Whoever believes in me, as the Scripture has said, streams of living water will flow from within him."

John 7:38

Murray Hack Photography

Murray Hack grew up on a farm near the town of Rocanville, Saskatchewan, Canada. He has been passionately seeking since he was a child. Following the completion of engineering at the University of Regina in 1999, his borders were expanded on a quest for the unknown. He has traveled across Canada, U.S., Mexico, Europe, Australia, Iceland, South America, and Antarctica. His expeditions have focused on viewing the natural beauty of this world.

Throughout this time, he began to hear God's voice speaking to him. He began to understand God's love. He learnt what he was living for- eternal salvation through Jesus Christ. Murray is a self taught photographer whose small business began through framed pictures in his home. God opened doors to sell photographs and this book for His purposes.

All proceeds from Murray Hack Photography go towards funding the many ministries of Souls Harbour RESCUE Mission.

Psalm 19:1-4 "The heavens declare the glory of God; the skies proclaim the work of his hands. Day after day they pour forth speech; night after night they display knowledge. There is no speech or language where their voice is not heard. Their voice goes out into all the earth, their words to the ends of the world."

Page	Name	Location	Date
2&3	Matthew 7:14	Iceland	June 21, 2003
4	2 Corinthians 4:6	Seljalandsfoss, Iceland	June 27, 2003
5	Romans 8:35	Drangajökull, Iceland	June 19, 2003
6	James 4:14	East Fjords, Iceland	June 23, 2003
7	Psalm 42:7	Skógafoss, Iceland	June 27, 2003
8&9	Acts 1:11	Vik, Iceland	June 25, 2003
10	1 Chronicles 16:27	Drangey, Iceland	June 20, 2003
11	Psalm 24:3	Drangey, Iceland	June 20, 2003
12	Proverbs 31:30	Drangey, Iceland	June 20, 2003
13	Job 28:11	Dynjandi, Iceland	June 19, 2003
14&15	Daniel 7:27	Vatnajökull, Iceland	June 24, 2003
16&17	Deuteronomy 32:2	Gullfoss, Iceland	June 25, 2003
18&19	Revelation 22:1	Hraunfossar, Iceland	June 18, 2003
20&21	Psalm 46:10	Kananaskis, Alberta, Canada	February 20, 2004
22&23	Psalm 50:2	Petermann Island, Antarctica	January 12, 2005
24	Jeremiah 9:6	Pleneau Island, Antarctica	January 12, 2005
25	Psalm 97:5	Pleneau Island, Antarctica	January 12, 2005
26&27	2 Corinthians 3:18	Lemaire Channel, Antarctica	January 12, 2005
28	Mark 15:38	Wilhelmina Bay, Antarctica	January 14, 2005
29	Job 37:10	Pleneau Island, Antarctica	January 12, 2005
30	Isaiah 9:2	Lemaire Channel, Antarctica	January 12, 2005
31	1 Thessalonians 5:5	Lemaire Channel, Antarctica	January 12, 2005

Page	Name	Location	Date
32&33	Revelation 21:11	Pleneau Island, Antarctica	January 12, 2005
34	1 Corinthians 15:55	Andvord Bay, Antarctica	January 13, 2005
35	Zechariah 14:7	Andvord Bay, Antarctica	January 13, 2005
36	James 1:12	Petermann Island, Antarctica	January 12, 2005
37	Matthew 7:24	Andvord Bay, Antarctica	January 13, 2005
38	Ephesians 3:12	Andvord Bay, Antarctica	January 13, 2005
39	John 18:36	Bailey Head, Antarctica	January 15, 2005
40	Ephesians 1:5	Petermann Island, Antarctica	January 12, 2005
41	1 John 5:4	Orne Island, Antarctica	January 14, 2005
42	Matthew 8:20	Bailey Head, Antarctica	January 15, 2005
43	Jeremiah 31:25	Hannah Point, Antarctica	January 15, 2005
44&45	Matthew 7:13-14	Andvord Bay, Antarctica	January 13, 2005
46&47	Psalm 78:26	Drake Passage	January 10, 2005
48	Psalm 104:26	Wilhelmina Bay, Antarctica	January 14, 2005
49	Job 9:8	Wilhelmina Bay, Antarctica	January 14, 2005
50	Job 12:10	Machu Picchu, Peru	January 6, 2005
51	Daniel 2:22	Glacier National Park, Argentina	January 25, 2005
52	Song of Solomon 4:10	Húsavík, Iceland	June 22, 2003
53	1 Timothy 1:18b-19	Ushuaia, Argentina	January 9, 2005
54	Psalm 75:10	Torres Del Paine National Park, Chile	January 25, 2005
55	Psalm 75:10	Torres Del Paine National Park, Chile	January 25, 2005
56&57	Ephesians 2:14	Glacier National Park, Argentina	January 20, 2005
58	Revelation 21:2	Torres Del Paine National Park, Chile	January 25, 2005

Page	Name	Location	Date
59	Matthew 21:21	Torres Del Paine National Park, Chile	January 25, 2005
60	Psalm 74:21	Torres Del Paine National Park, Chile	January 24, 2005
61	Zephaniah 1:15	Torres Del Paine National Park, Chile	January 25, 2005
62&63	Matthew 13:44	Machu Picchu, Peru	January 6, 2005
64	Matthew 3:16	El Calafate, Argentina	January 19, 2005
65	Isaiah 61:11	East Fjords, Iceland	June 23, 2003
66	Job 14:2	Rocanville, SK, Canada	December 27, 2003
67	Song of Solomon 2:12	Rocanville, SK, Canada	December 27, 2003
68	Numbers 21:17	Ushuaia, Argentina	January 18, 2005
69	Psalm 71:3	Lake Louise, AB, Canada	August 22, 2003
70	Isaiah 63:13	Rocanville, SK, Canada	December 24, 2003
71	Isaiah 44:22	Lake Louse, AB, Canada	August 22, 2003
72	Proverbs 15:17	Rocanville, SK, Canada	October 10, 2005
73	Psalm 119:111	Rocanville, SK, Canada	July 2, 2004
74	Ezekiel 31:7	Rocanville, SK, Canada	December 27, 2003
75	John 7:38	Surshellir and Stefanshellir Caves, Iceland	June 17, 2003